ReMind™

Building Rocks *of* Mindfulness
with Stepping Stones

Mara M. Zimmerman

Balboa Press books may be ordered through booksellers or by contacting:

Balboa Press
A Division of Hay House
1663 Liberty Drive
Bloomington, IN 47403
www.balboapress.com
844-682-1282

Interior Image Credit: Mara M. Zimmerman

ISBN: 979-8-7652-3818-9 (sc)
ISBN: 979-8-7652-3816-5 (e)

Library of Congress Control Number: 2023900968

Print information available on the last page.

Balboa Press rev. date: 04/13/2023

A guided meditation journey

Welcome

Sit quietly,

be still.

Good posture,
balanced breathing.

Be present,
be calm,
be cool.

Tune in,
tune out,
tune back in.

Imagine.

Peace.

Inner peace,
world peace,
peace of mind.

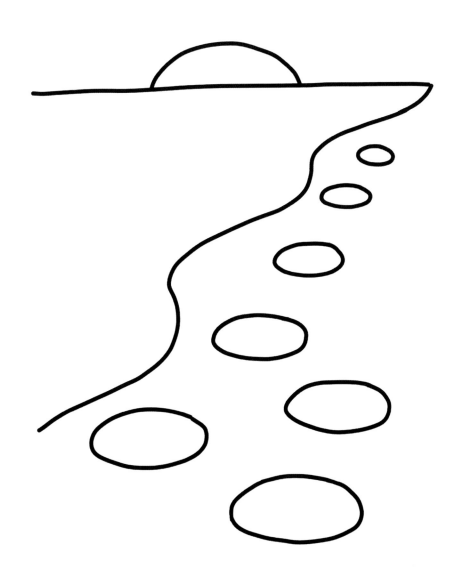

Intention,
attention.

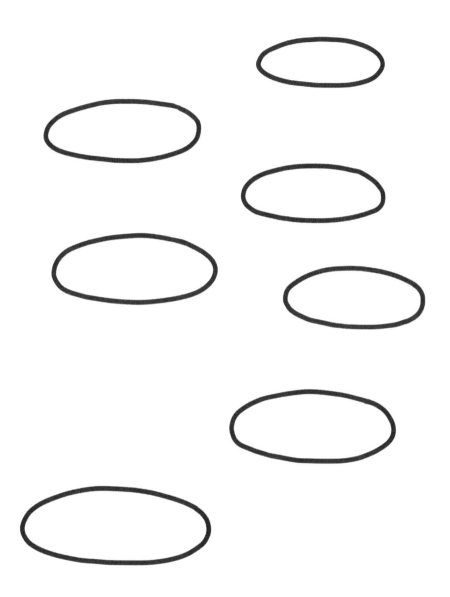

Be grounded, responsible, ready.

You got this.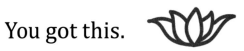

Breathe

Breath of life,
actions, choices.

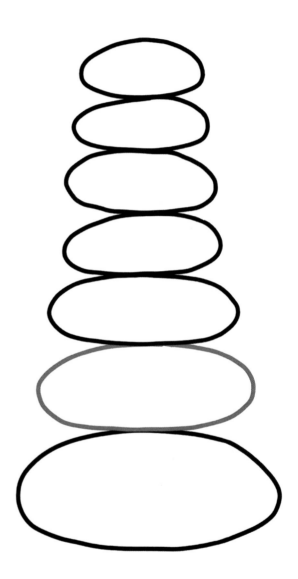

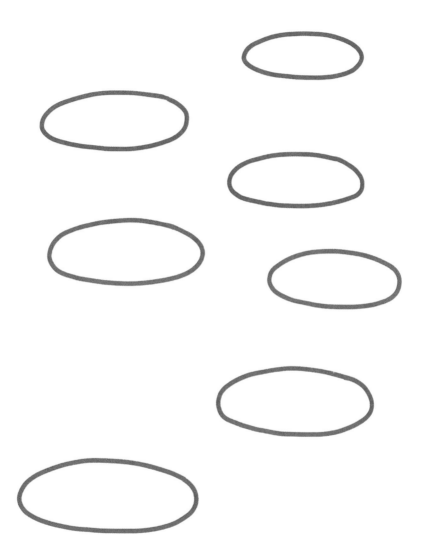

Happiness, enjoyment, effort, movement.

Laugh, play, dance, smile.

Breathe

Restore,
energize.

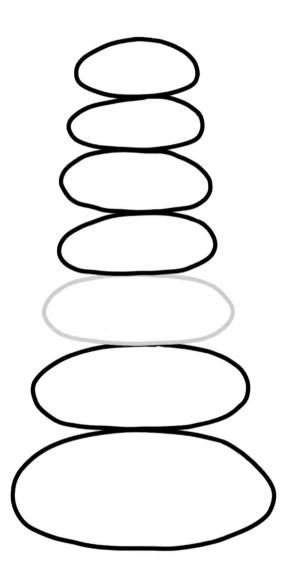

Pause, balance, center, inner sunshine.

Rest, reflect, recharge.

Breathe

Loving-kindness,
gratitude.

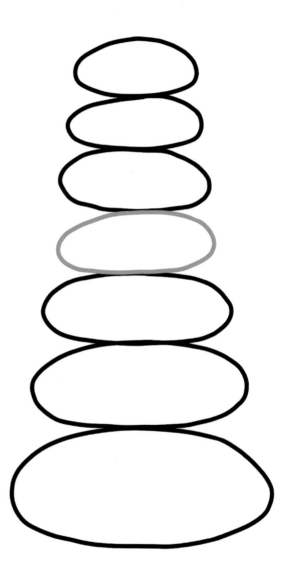

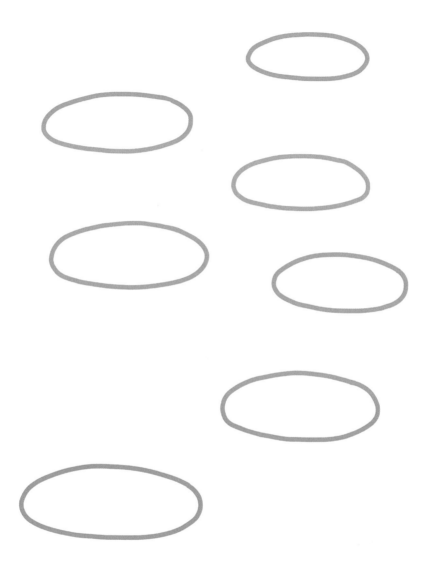

Heart centered, self-care, compassion.

Courage, creativity, giving, receiving.

Breathe

Communication,
community,

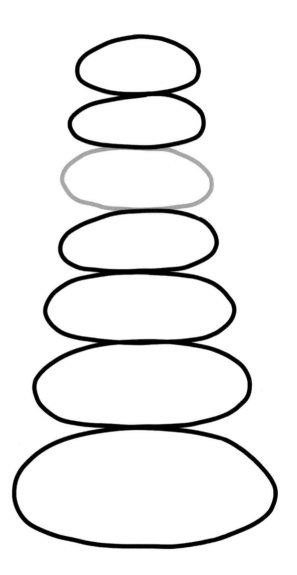

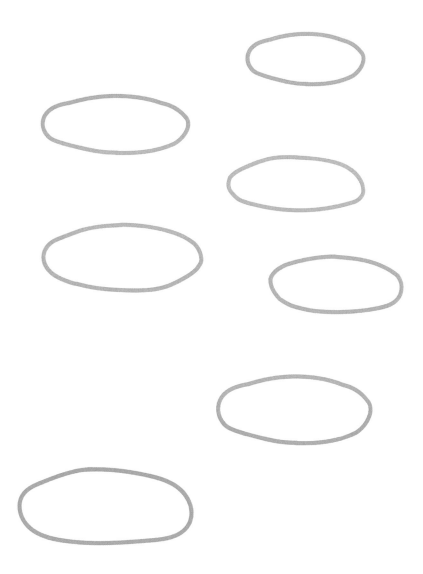

Nature, inner nature, sound, silence.

Prayers, blessings, songs, wishes.

Breathe

Quieting the mind,
calm.

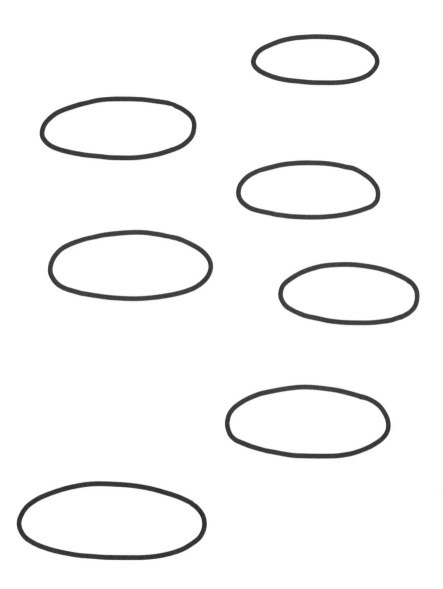

Imagination, feelings, positive thinking.

Knowledge, wisdom.

Breathe

Spiritual, soulful,
universal, personal.

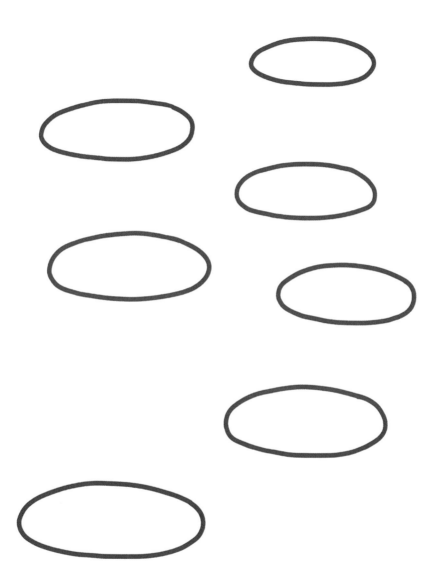

Gifts, talents, meaning, purpose.

Higher power, higher self.

Breathe

Start

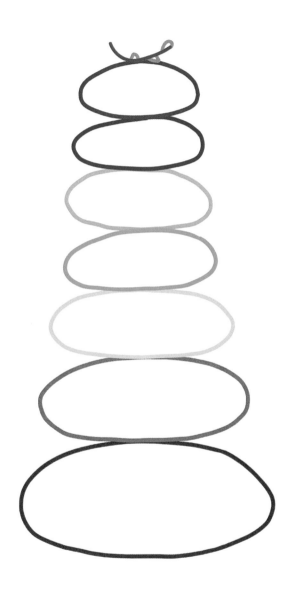

Restart

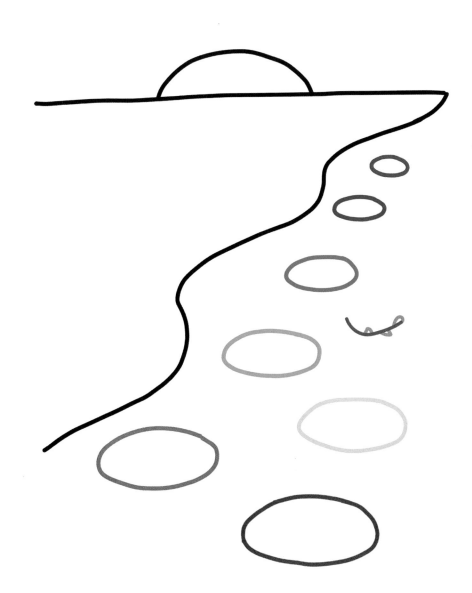

ReMind

About the Author

Mara M. Zimmerman has been teaching meditation and mindfulness to all ages in educational and therapeutic spaces throughout her career. She is the author of *ReMind: Building Rocks of Mindfulness with Jewish Stepping Stones,* and *How to Meditate and Why.*

For more information please visit
maramzimmerman.com

Printed in the United States
by Baker & Taylor Publisher Services